Après Moi, Le Dessert

A French Eighteenth Century Model Meal

Other books written, edited and/or translated by Jim Chevallier:

- *The Monologue Bin: Original Monologues for Teens and Adults*
- *Monologues for Teens and Twenties*
- *Views of Africa: Cameroon*
- *Views of California: the Redwoods*
- *Memoirs of the Bastille* by Simon-Nicolas-Henri Linguet
- *Edgar Allan Poe Analyzes Handwriting: A Chapter On Autography*
- *How To Cook A Peacock: Le Viandier - Medieval Recipes by Taillevent*
- *The Old Regime Police Blotter I: Bloodshed, Sex and Violence in Pre-Revolutionary France*

Work in other publications:

- Essay on "The Queen's Coffee and Casanova's Chocolate: The Early Modern Breakfast in France" in *Consuming Culture in the Long Nineteenth Century: Narratives of Consumption, 1700-1900* by Narin Hassan and Tamara S. Wagner
- Selected monologues included in *Millennium Monologs: 95 Contemporary Characterizations for Young Actors* and *Young Women's Monologs From Contemporary Plays: Professional Auditions For Aspiring Actresses* by Gerald Lee Ratliff
- Photographs of the wine makers of Chablis in *The Wines of Chablis and the Yonne* by Rosemary George.

Après Moi, Le Dessert:

A French eighteenth century model meal

Notes and translation by Jim Chevallier

Chez Jim Books • North Hollywood, CA

Published by:
Chez Jim Books

To contact the editor, e-mail: *jimchev@chezjim.com*

ISBN 1434829855

Table of Contents

The Meal

The following, somewhat theoretical, menu is for a meal to be served to 10-12 guests. It appears, in slightly different forms, in the 1705, 1714 and 1717 editions of the *Nouveau Cuisinier Royal et Bourgeois,* one of the most popular cookbooks of the eighteenth century (both in French and in various, not always credited, English translations). It is a relatively modest meal – relative, that is to most period menus which have survived and which tend to be for special meals served to royalty. This is meant, certainly, for a household of some means – enough to have a significant kitchen staff – but not necessarily one at the highest reaches of pre-Revolutionary French society.

To start with, it only consists of three services. One held for Marie-Antoinette included six, including sixteen entrées; Bonnefons lists eight in *Les Délices de la Campagne* (Amsteldam [sic], 1655). The three here are:

FIRST SERVICE

Centerpiece:	1 oille
6 entrées:	1 terrine of partridge with cabbage
	1 terrine of duck filets with green purée
	1 pigeon tart
	2 chickens in galantine
	1 larded filet of beef with cucumbers
	1 grenade with blood
2 hors-d'oeuvres:	Quail in the frying pan
	Small chickens in cinders, with ham essence on it

SECOND SERVICE

Centerpiece:	1 small quarter of veal, larded and served in its juice
4 roasts:	1 hen garnished with chickens with eggs

1 hen

4 young rabbits

1 plate of young pheasants garnished with
  young quail

4 hors-d'oeuvres: 2 salads

2 sauces

THIRD SERVICE

Centerpiece: 1 partridge paté or 1 wild boar head

6 medium dishes: 1 Noailles omelet

1 dish of fried cream, garnished with peach
  beignets

1 stew of green truffles

1 dish of artichokes

1 dish of peas

1 stew of crayfish tails

2 hors-d'oeuvres: 1 dish of fried animelles

1 dish of ramekins

Le Nouveau Cuisinier Royal et Bourgeois (1714), cited in
Alfred Franklin, *La Vie Privée d'Autrefois* (VI-"Les Repas":68-
71) (This collection incorporates additional data from the 1705
and 1717 editions.)

A fourth service is assumed here: the dessert (often composed of
fruit, fresh or in jellies or compotes).

One speaks of a table served in four services. The first are the
Entrées, the second the roast, the third the Entremets, & the
fourth, the Fruit, also called the Dessert.
Briand, *Dictionnaire des alimens, vins et liqueurs*, 1750 (III:389)

For an earlier menu (or, as the English said then, "Bill of Fare"),
the author of the *Cuisinier Royal* says of the dessert service: "It is
the Fruits & Jellies, which we will excuse ourselves from
discussing, since it is a matter for a Confectioner, rather than a
Cook." (5, 1705 ed.)

For each service all the dishes were put on the table together, sometimes being removed long enough to be carved and served. Though *service* is sometimes translated as "course", it was somewhat different, part of an overall approach referred to as "*Service à la Française*". While elegant in appearance, this had its disadvantages, as explained in the *Larousse Gastronomique* (1961; 874)

> It is easy to understand how overloaded were the tables if to these covered dishes are added the great tables centres, baskets of flowers, candelabras full of candles, set places, glass, etc. But the greatest inconvenience of this service, almost inevitably, was that in spite of the *réchauds,* the last dishes of the series, however great the dexterity of the carving and the speed of serving had become chilled, and no longer at their best. Moreover, it is equally evident that the guests could not try such a large number of dishes and must make choice of one or two.

Only some of the dishes listed for this model meal are described in the cookbook itself, and so most of the recipes provided here come from other cookbooks of the time. Some correspond to the exact item listed in the model menu, others are for similar dishes. The degree of detail provided for each item varies widely, depending on the recipes available, the familiarity of the item to modern readers, etc.

Ingredients

For urban cooks, the biggest obstacle here will be the use of game birds for a number of these recipes. These can certainly be obtained, but supermarket shoppers may want to resort to substitutes such as chicken or turkey. Otherwise, most ingredients used here can be found readily enough today (even, if you use the Web, testicles). Just a few will post a problem for the average cook.

Expense aside, many consumers object to how foie gras is produced. A similar reaction may apply to using coxcombs, which were once a common cooking ingredient. Luckily, even in the eighteenth century, it seems that some preferred to use a substitute:

> To make artificial Coxcombs. *From Mr. Renaud.*
>
> Take Tripe, without any Fat, and with a sharp Knife pare away the fleshy part, leaving only the brawny or horny part about the thickness of a Cock's Comb. Then, with a Jagging-Iron, cut Pieces out of it, in the shape of Cocks Combs, and the remaining Parts between, may be cut to pieces, and used in Pyes, and serve every whit as well as Cocks Combs: but those cut in form, please the Eye best; and, as Mr. *Renaud* observes, the Eye must be pleased, before we can taste any thing with Pleasure. And therefore, in Fricassees we should put those which are cut according to Art.
> Richard Bradley, *The Country Housewife and Lady's Director,* 1728

A nineteenth century writer says that most "coxcombs" served then were actually made from beef palate. Otherwise, sticklers for authenticity may be able to find them in ethnic markets.

Truffles were used very casually and very frequently in eighteenth century French recipes, simply, it seems because they did not become at all rare until much later. In some cases here, morels or other less expensive mushrooms may provide a substitute. Otherwise, modern cooks often use truffle paste (found on-line) or truffle oil for the taste.

Some ingredients used by eighteenth century cooks themselves required recipes. Two recipes here use a partridge coulis, one of many coulis used in eighteenth century cooking. Though English cookbooks of the period used the word "cullis", today the French word is commonly used in English for any number of purées, typically made from fruits or vegetables, while the eighteenth century versions were often meat-based.

Here are two period recipes for coulis', one "simple" and the other for partridge:

Simple coulis

Melt in a pot a little good butter, or melted lard. Put flour in it & cook it softly over the fire, until it is almost a roux. Take your pot off the fire; put in bouillon, meat juice or water. Stir it all well, bring it to a gentle boil, & put in a bouquet of parsley & spring onion, salt & a few sliced mushrooms. One can put in some braising stock & white wine, if desired. Skim & strain through the strainer. Be sure it is very smooth.
Marin, *Dons de Comus, ou L'Art de la Cuisine,* Paris, 1758 (I:13)

Partridge Coulis

Beat in a mortar two roast partridges with the strips of lard in which they have been cooked; put in a pinch of green truffles, & as many cooked mushrooms in melted lard, with fines herbes, spring onion, basil, marjoram; mix the pounded meat together in the same pot; add two spoonfuls of veal juice; let simmer on a low fire, & then strain through the strainer.
Dictionnaire des Alimens, Vins et Liqueur, Paris, 1750 (II:552-553)

The second recipe uses veal juice. In referring to meat, the French word *jus* can variously refer to gravy or to actual juice, as described here:

Beef Juice

Take a piece of Beef without any fat, cut it into slices, & put it in a terrine or little jar, which you will put on a bit of fire, after having closed it well … let your meat sweat this way for two hours, then take the juice that comes out of to use in stews or other things…

One can do the same thing to draw out the juice of Mutton & of Veal, or else half roast them on a spit, & press them in a press. *L'École Parfaite des Officiers de Bouche*, Paris, 1737 (422-423)

What makes this an 18th Century meal?

At first glance, few of these recipes will appear overtly exotic to a modern Western reader. What then makes them distinctly eighteenth century in nature?

To understand the answer, it helps to know not only how this cuisine differs from that in France today, but how it differs (or in some ways does not) from what came several centuries before it. Medieval cooking in France (as recorded for the more privileged classes) had several distinct characteristics:

- Large game birds, such as heron, peacock, stork, and swan, were standard fare; eighteenth century cooking still used a great deal of game, but generally smaller birds such as partridge, pheasant and quail.
- Beef (common in the eighteenth century) was rarely mentioned.
- "Oriental" spices, such as ginger, nutmeg, coriander and nutmeg, were commonly used for main courses; pepper was included with these, but on an equal footing. In the eighteenth century, the same spices were still used more (for main courses) than they would be in the twentieth century, but separately, while the pairing of salt and pepper was already standard.
- Duke's powder – essentially a mix of the same spices listed above – was standard. It does not appear in eighteenth century recipes.
- The frequent use of this limited set of very strong spices meant that many recipes tasted much alike; the distinction between eighteenth century dishes was already far more pronounced.
- Meat was often "redone" or restored by blanching or searing it before cooking it. This term rarely appears in

eighteenth century cookbooks.

- Verjuice was commonly used to moisten and flavor dishes. It was still common in the eighteenth century, but lemon juice and vinegar were used as frequently.
- Salads were not mentioned; eighteenth century cookbooks treat them as standard fare.
- Pea purée, often thickened with toasted bread, was frequently used as a binding. In the eighteenth century, egg yolks were normally used for this, as well as flour.

The roots of eighteenth century cuisine in medieval cooking still peeked through, then, but were not obvious. On the other hand, though in many ways eighteenth century cuisine was already more "modern", it differed from the French cuisine of the last hundred years in several key ways:

- Potatoes and tomatoes were effectively absent (though the potato became accepted towards the end of the century).
- Cucumbers were often served cooked (playing the roles later played by potatoes and tomatoes).
- Lettuce was often cooked.
- Salads included greens, such as glasswort, stonecrop and salad burnet, not generally used today.
- Garlic, though certainly used, was in no way characteristic of French cuisine.
- Ground spices like nutmeg were often paired with herbs like tarragon.
- Oil was little used for cooking and was even, when cooked, considered somewhat unhealthy (as opposed to all that wholesome butter and lard).

Anyone determined to be absolutely authentic should also bear in mind that this cooking was done not on a single stove, combining a broiler, an oven, and often a rotisserie with burners or hot plates, but in separate hearths and ovens, etc., as needed. Metaphorically, an eighteenth century kitchen (in a well-off household) was more like an orchestra, with separate, specialized sections, while today's kitchen offers the equivalent of a piano, or even a church organ, to a single cook.

Using These Recipes

It is entertaining to imagine a cook or club so devoted to eighteenth century cooking that they actually prepare every one of these dishes and serve them in the order indicated. (Your editor welcomes invitations to any such effort.) Most modern households however will find matter in these recipes for a number of separate meals.

Those reluctant to inflict an all-eighteenth century meal on their friends or family might simply slip in a promising dish and see how it is received. Few of these dishes are especially exotic and several, on the page, appear quite appetizing.

Hopefully, too, this collection will inspire some to their own inventions, using the particular combinations of ingredients which make these recipes eighteenth century in nature. (As it is, the minimal use of measurements allows for significant latitude even when following the original recipes.) Surely some diners would welcome a Neo-Eighteenth Century Nouvelle Cuisine?

Measurements

Though fairly detailed, these recipes were written long before exact measures were standard, and so the general absence of measurements is not so surprising as their occasional appearance. Here are the ones that appear in this collection:

- **Litron** – This was equal to a little more than an English pint.
- **Pint** – A French pint was equal to almost two English pints; in the original French, another measure appears, a *chopine*, which was nearly equivalent to an English pint. For simplicity's sake, all references here are to English

pints; when two pints are indicated, the original was probably a French pint.

- **Septier** – When used for liquids, this was also roughly equal to an English pint.

It should be noted that, before the Revolution, weights and measures were notoriously non-standard from one region to the next. Presumably the original cookbooks here, being for general use, referred to those of Paris.

Wines

Old Regime cookbooks did not suggest wines to match specific dishes. For anyone who wants to choose "appropriate" wines for an eighteenth century meal, however, hints can be found. For royalty, it seems, the choice was simple: champagne – bearing in mind that champagne was, for a long time, red and still. The sparkling version appeared in about 1700, but also fell out of favor under Louis XV (Alfred Franklin, *La Vie Privée d'Autrefois,* 1889 (VI–"Les Repas":137-138). So sticklers for historical accuracy will want to research the matter further.

Burgundy in general was popular, notably, the wine of Beaune, which was often suggested as a rival to champagne. (Many wines still considered superior today, such as Hermitage, Haut Brion, Chateau Margaux and Chateau Lafite, though already admired – and expensive –, were mentioned less frequently.)

For a more specific example, when the town fathers of Abbeville held several dinners in 1762, they drank wines of Beaune, Chablis, Champagne, and Volnay, as well as sweet Muscat from Lunel. (Ernest Prarond, *Abbeville à Table, études gourmandes et morales,* 1878, 57-66.) A similar selection might be considered for the meal described here.

First Service – Soups and Entrées

> Very few people are unaware of what we call, in Cooking terms, an Entrée; nonetheless, to give some idea of what it is, we will say that it is a sort of Dish, which is served immediately after the Soup, & before all other Dishes. Roasts are rarely served as Entrées; but often items from the oven, as Tourtes... and Pates...; Stews, Hashes, Gribelettes, white boudin, Andouillettes, Sausages, Beef a la Mode, Fricassées & other such Meats that can be served warm, ordinarily make up the Entrées of good Tables, because cold meats are rarely served as Entrées.
> (3, 1705 ed.)

The soup in this case is the oille, which might as easily be considered a stew. Some of the other dishes, such as terrines, would be served cold today, but were served warm at the time.

The Layouts

The original cookbook provides a basic layout for setting out the dishes in each service, but is not very specific as to what went where. The following diagram, like those that precede the subsequent services, indicates one possible arrangement of the dishes, based on hints in the work itself, similar examples in other works and plain guesswork. It omits a number of smaller, unidentified dishes grouped around the central dish. In one English example, these are shown as containing various game birds, but that may reflect specifically English taste. A French image of a meal much like this one shows no such dishes at all.

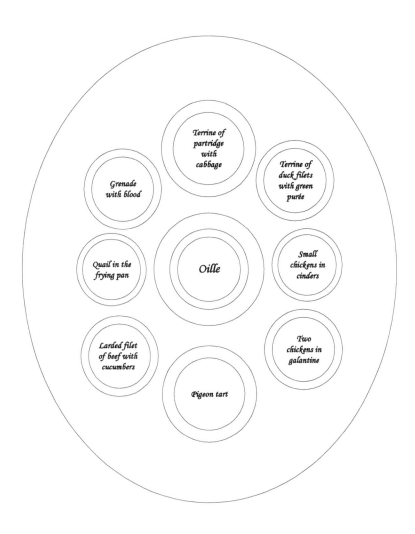

Centerpiece: Oille

The first dish listed - the centerpiece of the first service - is a once-popular dish called *Oille* (or *Oil*). A rough English pronunciation of this word is.... "Oy" - thereby freeing punsters to say things like, "An *oy* for an *oille*". (If you prefer an English word, this appears to be the same as the English "olio".) The *Nouveau Cuisinier* itself offers this recipe for what sounds like a particularly rich stew, or, with its ginger and nutmeg, like a medieval brewet:

> Take all sorts of good meats; that is, Beef from the haunch, filet of veal, a piece of leg of lamb, Duck, Partridge, Pigeons, Quail, a piece of raw Ham, Sausages & a Cervelas; brown all this in butter, put it in the pot, each thing according to the time it takes to cook, & make a liaison of your browned butter [*roux*] which you will put together with it. After having skimmed it well, season it with salt, clove, pepper, nutmeg, coriander, ginger, all of it well grated with thyme & basil, wrapped in a cloth. Then add all sorts of herbage & well-blanched root vegetables, as you prefer, such as onions, leeks, carrots, parsnip, parsley roots, cabbage, turnips and other in bundles. You must have tubs, silver stewpots, or other appropriate basins, & your soup being well boiled down, break crumbs up into pieces & let them simmer in the same broth well-skimmed and of a good flavor. Once simmered, before serving it add lots more broth, always well-skimmed: lay out your poultry & other meats, & garnish it with roots if you only have one basin; otherwise serve it without roots, putting the serving bowl on a silver platter & a silver ladle inside with which each can take some soup when the Oille is on the table.
>
> (329, 1705 ed.)

Six entrées

Terrine of partridge with cabbage

A terrine is an earthenware pot, most often round, it seems, in the eighteenth century. In earlier times, the term also referred to a chamber pot (hopefully the two uses were not confused.) It was also a type of cooked dish.

Today, if you order a terrine, it will be hard to distinguish from a paté, served in an elongated earthenware pots. The *Larousse Gastronomique* says firmly this must be served cold. But the Old Regime terrine was closer to a stew, and served hot (a crock pot, or the dishes served in crockery in some Asian restaurants, might be considered modern equivalents). It may be that, over the years, cooks discovered that the dish improved when left to cool and settle.

Though the *Nouveau Cuisinier Royal et Bourgeois* lists this as the first entrée in the first service, it only includes one recipe for a terrine per se:

TERRINE

What is called a Terrine, is a very substantial Entrée: here is what it is. One must have six Quail, four young Pigeons, two Chickens & a Quarter of Mutton cut into pieces. Set this to cook on the coals in a terrine, on a low fire, with bards of larding fat in the bottom, to keep it from burning; or small lard cut into pieces. Once cooked, skim off the grease, & put in its place good Veal juice, blanched & cooked hearts of lettuce, a little purée of green peas, with peas or asparagus tips. Let them cook together a bit longer, & only serve after skimming well.
(465, 1705 ed)

A nineteenth century dictionary, the *Dictionnaire General de la Cuisine Ancienne et Moderne* (1853), offers this recipe for "old" –

meaning eighteenth century? - style terrine (485):

> *Terrine in the old style* - Cook a plump chicken, a partridge,
> the saddle of a hare, a rump of veal and a rump of mutton in
> bouillon, all larded with moderately thick lard seasoned with
> fines herbes and spices. Let all this boil together. Then peel
> grilled chestnuts, clean them properly and put them to cook with
> the meat. Close the terrine tightly and seal it with firm dough so
> that all this cooks in its juices. Skim the fat off the sauce before
> serving it and then add in a glass of Canary wine.

These recipes give a good idea of the old version of a terrine.
None of these works offers one specifically for partridge with
cabbage, but the combination otherwise occurs frequently. The
following recipe might do perfectly well on its own, but could
also be adapted to a terrine:

Partridge with Cabbage

> Take three old partridges; after having cleaned them, truss
> them like chickens; lard them with large strips of lard, seasoned
> with salt, pepper, fine spices, grated and strained aromatics,
> parsley and chopped spring onions; line a pot with some bits of
> veal, two carrots, two onions and a half-clove of garlic; put your
> partridges on it, cover them with bards of larding fat; pour some
> good bases over them, or some bouillon or consommé; put your
> casserole on the fire, take it off; cover it with a round of buttered
> paper, as well as its cover; put it on the work surface, with fire
> under it and hot cinders on it; let it cook an hour or an hour and a
> quarter; then prepare the cabbage [*see below for preparation*], in
> which you will cook a cervalat and a piece of small lard; pare
> thirty red carrots, as many turnips; give them the diameter of a
> one franc piece (their length must be of the height of the mold I
> am going to mention); blanch these vegetables; drain them and
> let them cook in consommé, with a pinch of sugar to remove the
> bitterness; having let your cervelat and your lard cool, take a
> mold; butter it; put in the bottom a round of white paper and a
> band of paper around your mold inside and of its height; cut your
> cervelat into pieces like coins and your lard into slices, the
> thickness of your cervelat; put in the center of the mold a piece
> of cervelat; arrange around it slices of your lard, and so garnish

the bottom of your mold with circles of lard and your pieces of
cervelat; lay out around your mold your sticks of carrots and
turnips, mixing them together and tightening them one against
the other; press your cabbages, garnish the bottom of your mold
with them, and continue to garnish the sides with them like a
kind of counter-mure, so to speak; leave a hollow in the middle
to put your partridges in; put them in the bottom on their
stomachs; fill your mold with cabbages, cutting back anything
that spills over, and press them down, in order to give them a
firm consistency, so that in turning out your partridges, your
decoration will not be disturbed; put a cover on this mold, and
keep your partridges warm in a double-boiler; strain their stock
through a silk strainer; add in three skimming spoons of worked
Spanish sauce...; let your sauce cool, skim it, reduce it to the
consistency of a demi-glace; turn your chartreuse over on your
dish, remove the paper, drain it carefully, tamp off the moisture,
as well as possible, with the corner of a cloth; sauce it with your
reduction, and serve.
Beauvilliers, *L'Art du Cuisinier,* Paris, 1814 (I, 275-277)

The cabbage can be prepared as in this dish, before adding the
cervelat and the lard:

Piece of Beef garnished with Cabbage

Take two or three cabbages; cut them into quarters; wash
them; blanch them: when done, let them cool: bind them; put
them in a stewpot; moisten them with bouillon. If you have stock
from braising or some other good stocks, use them; add in some
carrots, two or three onions, including one stuck with three
cloves, a garlic clove, laurel, thyme; what is more, so that your
cabbage are well filled out, add it in the last of your stewpot; let
them simmer three or four hours; drain them on a white cloth;
squeeze them to get the grease out in giving them the form of a
rolling pin. Lay them out and your piece of meat, cover them,
like your cabbage, with a reduced Spanish sauce, and serve.
(108-109)

Spanish sauce is described under "Two sauces" in the second
service. Note too that the first recipe references bouillon and
consommé in several forms, including a base. These were

common elements to prepare and keep on hand for use in dishes; recipes for them could fill a separate volume. Here is one recipe for a base:

Ordinary bouillon, or simmering for the base of soups and sauces

This bouillon must be made with all possible care. Take the required quantity of meat. The best is the top round, bottom round and upper leg of beef. Add in a chicken or a veal shank. When it has been well skimmed, salt it lightly and put in appropriate root vegetables, such as turnips, carrots, parsnip, onions, celery & leeks, with a clove & a parsley root. This bouillon or simmering is used to cook everything put on soups, such as fowl, game, large meat, &c. & all the garnishes or vegetables, except cabbage, radishes, & some other vegetables...A part of the goodness of all bouillons depends on the attention & care taken.

Dons de Comus (I:2-3)

Terrine of filet of duck with green sauce

Recipes for soup sometimes doubled as recipes for sauce. The following recipe could be used for a green sauce, letting it boil down a bit more:

Green soup

Take the yolks of hard-boiled eggs, cooked poultry livers, & chestnuts, crush all this together in a mortar with parsley or sorrel & Swiss chard. add in bouillon, or water, salt, powdered cinnamon & other spices, then cook them sufficiently & make a soup of it.
La Varenne, *Le Cuisinier François* (12)

Otherwise, here is a straightforward recipe for a green sauce:

Green sauce

Take green wheat on the stalk, blanch it, chop it up and grate it; put in a pot a spoonful of good bouillon, a crust of bread, two or three cloves of garlic, a half-glass of vinegar, salt, pepper. Simmer and strain with the wheat. This must have the consistency of a double cream. One can also make this with parsley or another green.
Les Dons de Comus (I:71)

The filet of duck can be prepared as follows:

Filet of duck á la Manselle

Take two or three hung and tender ducks. Pluck them & restore [*that is, blanch or brown*] them. Put them on the spit & half-cook them. Take them off & cut the stomachs of your three ducks. Be careful not to lose the juice which comes out. Take off the skins & score them up lengthwise. Chop up in a casserole a pinch of shallots, a truffle, a foie gras, salt, pepper, a half-spoonful of white veal stock, half a glass of wine, two spoonfuls of oil. Boil all this for a quarter of an hour. Put in your duck fillets, & keep them on hot cinders. They must not boil; when serving, [add] lemon juice.
Les Dons de Comus (II, 243-244)

The above can be cooked in a terrine as explained in the previous article, and served with a green sauce.

Pigeon tart

This is one of the simpler dishes listed, especially if one omits the godiveau and the coxcombs:

Pigeon tart

Line your tart dish with large greens with a little godiveau in the base. Take small pigeons, scald & truss them the feet inside. Then put them in a pot with grated lard, very white mushrooms, garnishes, like cooked and blanched coxcombs, blanched sweetbreads of veal or lamb & other such things. Strain it all a minute, & season with salt, pepper, nutmeg, a bouquet [of herbs]. When this is cold, garnish your tart, cover as normal, finish, gild, & cook as needed; then skim and pour in white veal stock.
Les Dons de Comus (III:84)

The *godiveau* mentioned at the start would be like the filling made for this "Paté de Godiveau":

Make a good Godiveau, with fillet of veal, beef marrow or fat, & a little lard; season with salt, pepper, cloves, nutmeg, fines herbes & spring onion: lay out your Paté on a fine dough base in the form you want, round or oval, & two or three fingers high: garnish it with mushrooms, sweetbreads, artichoke hearts, morels & chitterlings in the opening in the center, & when serving pour a white sauce over it.
(341-342, 1705 ed.)

Chickens in galantine

The *Cuisinier Royal et Bourgeois* itself offers a rather appetizing recipe for suckling pig in galantine, but nothing for chicken. This recipe is from the celebrated "Gifts of Comus":

Chicken in galantine

Pluck and debone entirely. Take out part of the flesh with which you will make an ordinary fine stuffing, well thickened. Stretch the skin of the chicken out neatly on a napkin. Put the stuffing on it, then arrange thin sticks of lard, pistachios, thin sticks of truffles & of ham, all well arranged and set well one against the other. Put the rest of the stuffing on top, a grain of salt & and other light seasonings. Roll your galantine up tightly, & wrapped in lardoons. Put in a white cloth. Roll & tie up the two ends. Cook on the fire & serve with whatever sauce you want. Can be served cold.
Les Dons de Comus (II, 109-110)

While the Merriam-Webster Online Dictionary says that a modern galantine is "a cold dish consisting of boned meat or fish that has been stuffed, poached, and covered with aspic", note that this eighteenth century version is neither covered in aspic nor necessarily served cold.

Filet of beef with cucumbers

Exceptionally, the *Cuisinier Royal et Bourgeois* supplies its own recipe for this dish. The use of cooked cucumbers as a side was common at the time and probably all the more important before potatoes and tomatoes became standard parts of French cuisine.

> *Entrée of Filet of Beef with Cucumbers*
>
> Take a very tender Filet of Beef; roast it, larded, & wrapped in paper; do not over-cook it. After cut it into thin small slices, & put them in a plate. Cut the Cucumbers into slices, according to the quantity of your Filets; they must be marinated; then squeeze them out, & put lard in a pot, to brown them well on the furnace. Then drain off all the lard, & put in a bit of flour, & strain it again a bit: after, moisten with good juice, according to the quantity of your Filets. Once cooked, put in a good binding: a spoonful of ham essence will work perfectly. Put in a trickle of verjuice, or of vinegar; & do not let your Filets boil more, because they will become hard. Serve them warm, garnished with fried bread, marinades, or rissoles.
>
> All other sorts of Filets with Cucumbers must be made in this way.
> (133-134, 1705 *ed.*)

Apparently the cucumbers are truly meant to be marinated here, and not pickled. But the only marinades in this cookbook are for meats. Probably the half-water and half-vinegar mixture with salt used for pickling could also be used – more briefly – for a marinade.

A grenade with blood

This recipe appeared in at least one edition of the *Nouvel Cuisinier Royal* itself and is given in Alfred Franklin's version of the meal.

Grenade in French means pomegranate and the name of this dish (like the similar grenadin) seems to play on the symmetry of a cut pomegranate:

Grenade

> To make a Grenade, you need several rumps of veal larded with small strips of lard, & a round pot that is not too big. Put some nice bards of larding fat underneath, and lay out your veal rumps with the lard outside; let them touch at the point in the middle, & let them touch one another, lest all that come apart while cooking; make them hold together with beaten egg white, in which one moistens the hand, to dampen by the edges, which must be thinner than the rest. Put in the hollow which this makes and all around a little farce of mirotons, reserving the middle. Take [the white meat from??] a fat hen, cooked partridges and pheasants, cut the white into little cubes, take about half a pound of the fat which you will cut into cubes seasoned with salt, pepper, fines herbes, fine spices. Take the blood of eight or ten pigeons; mix this meat and the fat cut into cubes with this blood. Put into your grenade, cover with godiveau and cook. Once cooked, reverse it, and having lifted the points of the rumps of veal, make a hole with the point of a knife, moisten it with ham essence or a little clear coulis of partridge and serve it hot.
> (I:360, 1714 ed., cited in Alfred Franklin's *Histoire de la Vie Privées* (VI:69)

The casual reference to a miroton above gives no hint that this tended to be a substantial dish in its own right. Here is one of several recipes for that dish:

Veal Miroton

Take a nice filet of veal, make of it several fine slices, which you will beat with the cleaver to flatten them; chop up other filets of veal with lard, beef marrow, mushrooms, truffles, fines herbes & good seasonings; put in two or three egg yolks, & a little bread crumb soaked in cream.

This stuffing being made garnish the bottom of a pot with neatly arranged bards of larding fat: then put in your beaten slices of veal, then the stuffing which you will cover with the rest of your slices, all of it well closed; then turn over your bards, cover everything well & put a gentle fire above & below it as to braise it [*alternately*, in hot coals]; the miroton being cooked skim it well, put it in the dish upside down, put in if you like a little mushroom coulis... & serve hot.
Dictionnaire des Alimens (II:343)

To make the mushroom coulis mentioned here, you must first make mushroom gravy or juice:

Mushroom juice

Your mushrooms being well-cleaned, put them in a pot with a lump of lard or butter; if it is for a meatless meal, brown them on the coals until they stick to the bottom of the pot; once well-browned, put in a little flour & brown it more with the mushrooms; then put in good bouillon with or without meat, & after bringing it to a boil once or twice, take it off the fire, & put this juice separately in a jar; season with salt & a piece of lemon, to use as needed.

Mushroom coulis

Take mushroom juice, soak bread crusts in it; when they are well-soaked, strain all this through the strainer to use when you need it.
Dictionnaire des Alimens (II:328-329)

Two hors-d'oeuvres

Hors-d'oeuvres in the eighteenth century sense were non-essential additions to the main meal:

> In cooking, hors-d'oeuvres refer to all the dishes served on a table, & which one could do without to have a complete meal. Hors-d'oeuvres are not served unless there are many dishes to serve, or else in a small meal to avoid [serving] Entrées which cost more.
>
> *Dictionnaire des Alimens* (II:153)

Quail in the frying pan

The first of the two hors-d'oeuvres is quail in the frying pan, which sounds simple enough, but, as seen below, could be fairly ornate. Also, one might readily think that something cooked "in the frying pan" would be fried, but that does not seem to be the case here.

Randle Cotgrave's French-English dictionary (1611) offers *paelle* as one alternative version of *poele (*frying pan*)*. Originally, this seems to have meant the kind of shovel that is used in a fireplace. It is easy to see this word's possible relation to a famous Spanish dish.

> *Quail in the frying pan*
>
> Split your quail along the back. Make a stuffing with grated lard, chopped raw ham, truffles, some foie gras, a raw egg yolk; all mixed, seasoned with salt, pepper, nutmeg and fines herbes; stuff your quail with this chopped mixture; stuff your pot with bards of larding fat, slices of veal & of ham. Close it carefully; sweat it over hot cinders for two hours. Take out the bards & the slices; finish cooking your veal on the stove. When they have started to brown, & the juice begins to stick to the pot; take them off; skim; moisten what remains stuck to the pot with bouillon and juice. Strain; add crushed pepper, lemon juice; pour on your quail. This method is given because pigeons, chickens, partridges in the frying pan are prepared the same way.
> *Dictionnaire Portatif de Cuisine, d'Office et de Distillation*, 1767 (105)

Chicken in cinders

This recipe is from the same work as the meal:

> Take two small chickens, truss them as for boiling... Take as many as you have of chickens of sheets of paper. Put each chicken on its sheet of paper, season them on top and underneath..... Tie it, moisten it in water and bury it in hot cinders, putting fire on it from time to time, letting it cook for two and half hours or three. When you think it cooked, take it out and unwrap it and lay it out on the plate. Pour over it ham essence, let it be flavorful and with some bite. Serve hot as an entrée or hors d'oeuvre.
> 1714 ed., quoted in Alfred Franklin's *Histoire de la Vie Privée (VI:"Repas"* :69)

Here is one recipe for ham essence:

Ham essence.

> Take very fine slices of raw ham and pound them with the handle of a knife; line the bottom of a pot with them that you will sweat on the furnace. When they stick put in a little melted lard; powder them with a little flour, stir with a spoon and moisten with veal juice; season with a bouquet of spring onions and fines herbes, a nail of clove, some slices of lemon, a handful of chopped mushrooms, chopped truffles, some bread crusts, and a trickle of vinegar. When all this is cooked, strain in a strainer and do not boil this juice any further.; use it for all kinds of things which contain ham; some put in a clove of garlic.
> *Dictionnaire des alimens, vins et liqueurs* (II:181)

Second Service - Roasts

This version of the Roasts service varies a bit from the general definition Massailot gives earlier:

> In proportion to the Entrees which one will have served, & of how many are at the Table, will be three large dishes, composed of all sorts of Game in the season; & four Salads in the corners. (7, 1705 ed.)

In this case, sauces replace two of the salads, and in fact there is less game than in the first service. The roasts may have been served cold.

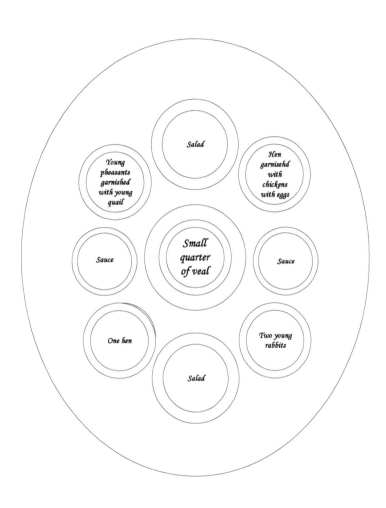

Centerpiece: A small quarter of veal, larded and served in its juice

This centerpiece begins the second service of this model meal. The dish sounds simple enough, but the *Nouvel Cuisinier Bourgeois et Royal* offers some nuances for both a quarter and the *longe* (top part of the loin) of veal:

For the Quarter & Loin of Veal

One can lard it with small strips of lard, except for the wide end, which is breaded well; let it have a good taste. Garnish it with rissoles of Capon whites, & veal juice over it when serving it.

You can also marinate it in an oval pot, well seasoned: and once cooked on the spit, take the kidneys to make stuffed roasts, with which you will garnish your Quarter of Veal; or else an omelet: & you garnish it with Cutlets or Chickens, or with stuffed Cutlets and fried parsley.

Another medium Entrée is made of half of a Loin of Veal cooked in a good well-seasoned, substantial court-bouillon, wrapping it in a napkin, lest it break. Garnish it with fried bread, parsley, zests of lemon.
(497-498, 1705 ed.)

Here is a recipe for the rissoles:

Rissoles for meat days

Make a hash of capon white meat or else a piece of veal blanched on the grill, parsley, spring onion, mushroom, a little cooked ham, a little bread crumb soaked in cream, two raw egg yolks as a binding; pound all this together in a mortar; make shells of very thin puff pastry. Make little pastry shells in which you will put about a walnut's size of your stuffing; cover it with the same dough, seal the two pastry shells tight; trim all around the rissole; then fry it in very hot refined lard.
Dictionnaire des Alimens (III:285-286)

Four Roasts

1 hen garnished with chickens with eggs

The first of four roasts for the second service of this model meal is "*1 poule garnie de poulets aux oeufs*"; the second is simply a "*poule*". It may come as a surprise to those who never think too hard about their poultry that a chicken is the young stage of either a hen or cock, and so, a *poule* and a *poulet* (hen and chicken) are in fact different, though a supermarket shopper may have to make do with one type of bird for both. Even eighteenth century cookbooks do not always make a distinction. With this, a third word – *poularde* – indicates a young fatted hen (not to be confused with a "plump chicken" - *poulet gras*).

If needed, a recipe for roast hen follows. The addition to that dish of "chickens with eggs" may refer to the following, somewhat more complex, preparation:

> *Plump chickens with small eggs*
>
> Hard boil the eggs, chop the yolks with parsley, spring onion, shallots, salt, pepper, basil, a little bread crumb simmered in cream, four raw egg yolks, a little beef marrow, all well grated together, & with a good taste. Make of them little eggs, like ordinary little eggs, flour & fry in refined lard that is light in color. They can be cooked in bouillon. Brown a little veal with mushrooms and a lump of butter. Singe and moisten with excellent bouillon. Once the veal is cooked, strain the sauce, pour in a binding of two egg yolks with a little chopped parsley, blended with bouillon, lemon juice, & pour in your little eggs without letting them boil further. Put these little eggs on whole chickens, cooked on the spit, or cut up, cooked in strips of lard.
> *Les Dons de Comus* (II:176-177)

These "eggs" sound like very tasty croquettes, and could probably be used with a number of dishes.

One hen

The general eighteenth century approach to roasting was fairly simple and consistent: lard the meat, truss it (if applicable) and roast it on a spit. Here is one recipe specifically for chicken, in this case, a *poularde* (fatted hen):

Fatted hen on the spit

Your fatted hen plumed and hung, empty it & blanch it on the fire. Then stub it clean; wrap it in bards of larding fat & truss it. Cook it on the spit. When it is almost cooked, take off the strips of lard, bread it with very fine crumbs; brown it nicely, & serve hot.

You can also lard your chicken with the same lard, cook it the same way, & serve it with lemon juice, & verjuice seasoned with salt & white pepper.

Dictionnaire des Alimens (III:116-117)

Four young rabbits

The following recipe for roast rabbit, from a book of "healthy cuisine", is not noticeably different from standard recipes for the time:

Roast young rabbits

The skinned young rabbit, must be interlarded with narrow strips of lard, & covered with a bard of larding fat; put it on the spit, baste it with its juice, & serve it accompanied with a spicy sauce or a pepper sauce in a saucer.

When it does not lose its juices in cooking, it is a delicate morsel, fine, & one of the healthiest; but it must not be over-cooked: I have constantly observed that they are more succulent when only barded, than when they are perfectly interlarded. Jourdan Le Cointe, *La Cuisine de Santé* (III:57)

Why, if the last line is true, the author starts by saying to interlard (*piquer*) the rabbit is not clear.

A plate of young pheasants garnished with young quail

Since this is listed as the last of four roasts for the second service, both the pheasant and the quail can assumed here to be roasted. Though basic roasting might not require an additional recipe, recipes exist for these birds separately which are a touch more ornate, even rather appetizing:

Roast pheasant

Let your pheasants hang more or less, according to taste & the season; pluck them, carefully remove all their down, & singe them lightly.

Compose a fine stuffing, with liver, parsley, shallots, grated lard, salt, pepper & nutmeg; chop all this carefully, & bind it with two egg yolks; fill your pheasants with it, without over-stuffing them, & put their button [*sic - not a standard culinary term*] in their croupe; fasten the thighs with a little silver needle or a wooden skewer, & bind it all around with a bit of new string.

Brown them with melted butter; wipe them well, & put one or two strips of lard in each one, or else stud them all around with firm little strips of lard, & moderately seasoned.

Put them on the spit, & cook them over a low fire, basting them frequently to cook them perfectly.

These are very esteemed roasts, & of a delicate & healthy succulence....

Roast quail

Pluck them, flame them, & brown them on a low fire; empty them & rub them with a little white fat on the whole body; cover them with two broad strips of lard, one on the back, the other under the belly; because quail tending to dry out must be well moistened to protect it from fire: put them on the spit, baste them & serve them as normally.

To give them a more agreeable odor, baste them on the spit with consommé in which two leaves of laurel have been boiled with some juniper seeds.

They are healthy & fine.

Jourdan Lecointe, *La Cuisine de Santé* (III:64-65; 77-78)

Quail being much smaller than pheasant, it is probably enough to distribute them around the larger bird as a garnish to obtain the dish listed here.

Four hors-d'oeuvres

Two salads

The second service ends with 4 hors-d'oeuvres, the first two simply indicated as "2 salads".

The lack of specifics on the salad, though not very helpful, is fairly typical for the period. Here and there recipes for salad do appear, but the general attitude of culinary authors seems to be, as below, that "Everybody knows how to make salads.". Luckily, the same source at least provides an overview of what was meant by a salad in France in our period:

> SALAD, *Aceteria*. Composed of different potager garden plants, normally eaten raw; they are seasoned with salt, vinegar & oil; it is thus that one makes a mix of head or loose-leaf lettuce with garnishes, for instance, balm, tarragon, chervil, salad burnet, purslane, &c. There are cooked salads, such as those one makes with beets; there are those preserved in salt & vinegar, such as those made with small cucumbers, otherwise called pickles, nasturtiums, capers, nasturtium buds, &c. Salads are also made of several fish.... Everybody knows how to make salads.

It seems from the above that even assorted pickles could be served as salads. The same article includes a recipe for a rather ungreen salad:

> *Salad of mixed meat*
>
> Take whichever flesh of poultry or game that you want to cook on the spit; cut your meat into fine strips arrange them neatly in patterns on a plate with chopped lettuce which you put in the bottom, the meat on it, & make patterns with salad herbs; if you do not want to put in salad, chop up parsley & spring onion very fine; arrange these fine herbes in patterns with the strips of meat, & serve seasoned with salt, coarse pepper, oil & vinegar.
>
> *Dictionnaire des alimens* (III, 314-315)

In general, what recipes do appear tend to be for ingredients other than the leafy vegetables typical of salad:

Artichokes in salad

Cook artichoke hearts, well pared and quite white. Once cooked drain them & arrange them on the plate. You can garnish them with coxcombs, shrimp tails, hearts of lettuce chopped fine, salad herbs. Rub the plate well with a little garlic, & season your salad with oil, salt, pepper, & a little Tarragon vinegar.
Les Dons de Comus (II:429)

For comparison's sake, here are two English recipes for salads from 1672:

45. *To make several Sallads, and all very good.*

Take either the stalks of Mallows, or Turnip stalks when they run to seed, or stalks of the herb Mercury with the seedy head, either of these while they are tender put into boiling Water and Salt, and boiled tender, and then Butter and Vinegar over them.

46. *To make a Sallad of Burdock, good for the Stone, another of the tender stalks of Sow-thistles.*

Take the inside of the Stalks of Burdock, and cut them in thin slices, and lay them in water one whole day, shifting them sometimes, then boil them, and butter them as you do the forenamed.

Also the tender Stalks of Sow-thistles done in like manner, are very good and wholesome.
Hannah Wolley, *The Queen-like Closet or Rich Cabinet Stored With All Manner Of Rare Receipts For Preserving, Candying And Cookery. Very Pleasant And Beneficial To All Ingenious Persons Of The Female Sex,* 1672

Two sauces

The last two items of the second service are two sauces. Not only are no specific sauces listed, but it is not clear if they are to be eaten directly (soups and sauces were sometimes made from the same recipe), sopped with bread or otherwise consumed.

Here are some recipes for several common sauces, much used in recipes of the time:

Spanish sauce

Sweat a piece of veal & zests of ham with some root vegetables. Make it stick a little & moisten it with veal juice, two glasses of garlic essence, two tablespoons of white veal stock, a glass of good oil, a pinch of coriander, two nails of clove, three or four whole mushrooms. Simmer over a low fire & skim off the oil. When the meat is cooked, strain the sauce through a strainer. It must have body and flavor. Once it has been strained, put in a few slices of lemon. It is used for many things.

Sauce Robert

Chop some onion up in thin slices, or in rounds, or in cubes. Brown it with butter, or melted lard over a low fire. When it is almost cooked, & it begins to take on color, singe it a little, & moisten it with juice and white veal stock, if you have any, season with salt & pepper, an onion studded with two cloves. Let simmer. In finishing, [add] a little mustard, a touch of vinegar.

Those who do not like onion can strain the sauce.

Sauce Robert Housewife Style

Chop a good quantity of onions up very fine, brown it in a frying pan or pot, with a lump of butter, or other shortening. Leave it a long time on the fire, & stir it often, so that it does not burn. When it is done, season it with salt, pepper; in finishing, some mustard & vinegar. It is not necessary to moisten it because the onion gives enough juice to cook it....

Green meadow sauce

Sweat in a pot slices of onion, some small slices of veal, a little ham, zests of carrot & parsnip. When this has released its juice, & begins to thicken, moisten with good bouillon, a glass of Champagne wine, a half-glass of oil. Put in two cloves of garlic studded with a clove nail. Let the sauce cook.

Strain it through a silk strainer to skim it. Put in a pot a half bar of Vanvre butter, with a little flour. Put in bouillon according to the sauce you need. Turn it on the fire, to give it body. Put in a good pinch of parsley, chopped & blanched, & chopped up again after, so that it forms the green meadow. In serving [add] lemon juice. This sauce can be served cold.

Dons de Comus (I:18-19, 33-34, 35-36)

Third Service – Entremets

Massailot does not provide a precise definition of this course, which was sometimes combined with the roasts in the second service. One French-English dictionary of the time defines them as "*Dainty dishes or plates*, such as are served at a great table just before the fruit." (M. A. Boyer, *Dictionnaire Royal François-Anglais, en Abrégé*, Lyon, 1783, 195). Such dainty dishes could include items – such as fried cream – that modern diners might think of as dessert, but also.... boar's head.

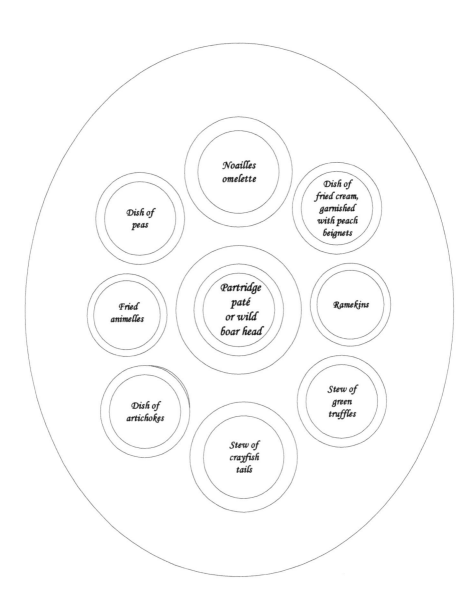

Centerpiece: partridge paté or boar's head

The third service for this model meal begins with a choice of two dishes as a centerpiece: a partridge paté or a boar's head.

The work's own recipe for the first is actually for a mix of partridge and snipe:

> *Warm Paté of Partridge, Snipe, etc.*
>
> Take two Partridges and two Snipe; the Partridges, clean them well & keep the liver; truss the one and the other neatly, & beat them on the stomach with a rolling pin: then stud them with large lardoons & ham seasoned with pepper & salt. Having larded them, split them along the back: make a stuffing with a piece of veal as large as an egg, very tender, with raw lard, a little marrow, some parsley & fines herbes, a little chopped truffle and mushroom, & some veal fat. All of it being well chopped up & seasoned, bind it with an egg yolk, & stuff your four pieces from the back. Then chop & grate lard; take the two Partridge livers, & grate them all together, & season that with fine spices. Make a Dough composed of an egg, of good butter & flour, & a little salt. Form two pastry crusts, lay one out on buttered paper; take lard grated in the mortar, & spread it out neatly on the pastry shell. Season your Partridges & Snipes, & lay them out roundly: you must have broken their bones. Put in some truffles & mushrooms, a laurel leaf, all well covered with strips of lard. Press your other pastry crust around: close the sides well all around, gild your Dough & put it in the oven, watching the fire. Once cooked, take it out & remove the paper from under it, take a good Partridge coulis, some sweetbreads, mushrooms & truffles; cut the cover of the Dough, remove all the strips of lard, skim it well, squeeze the juice of a lemon; & when serving, pour it all in the Paté very hot, cover it & serve at the same time as an Entrée.
>
> (337-339, 1705 ed.)

The *Dictionnaire des Alimens* gives a very similar recipe, using only partridge.

For the alternate recipe, you can also use a pig's head.

Boar's Head Entremets

Take the Head, & singe it well with a clear fire; then rub it with a piece of brick, vigorously, to remove the bristle. You will finish scraping with the knife, & clean it as needed. After that, debone it, taking out the two jaws & the muzzle: split it underneath, so that it stays attached on top with its skin: & you will take out the brain & the tongue. Take your knife, & using the point insert salt in all the flesh. Then you will put it back and join it together, & tie it up well, wrapping it in a napkin. You must have a big kettle, with a large quantity of water, all sorts of fines herbes, pork belly, coriander: two laurel leaves, anise, clove & cracked nutmeg, & salt, if you think there is not enough. Then onion & rosemary are needed: & when half-cooked, put in a bottle of good wine, & finish cooking it for twelve hours.

One can also cook the tongue in the same bouillon. If you have time, you can leave the same head in its salt, & salt it before cooking it. Once cooked, let it cool in its bouillon; then take it out, lay it neatly in its dish, & serve it cold, whole or in slices. (267-268)

Six medium dishes

Omelet à la Noailles

A recipe for an omelet "Noailles Style" appears in the corresponding (1715) edition of the same work, but it is not said which member of the prominent Noailles family gave the recipe its name. The Noailles name reappears through hundreds of years of French history: to cite just two examples, Louis, duke de Noailles, was captain of the Life Guards when Damiens stabbed Louis XV in 1757, and in the early twentieth century poet Anna de Noailles was an intimate of Proust (and so Proustians might also want to serve this dish.)

This "omelet" seems more like a soufflé:

> Take a pint of milk; put in a pot a silver spoonful of rice flour, a little salt; work this flour with a drop of milk, and put in it eight fresh egg yolks, and blend them well with the rest of the pint of milk; add in a half septier of sweet cream, and put in a piece of stick cinnamon and sugar in proportion, and cook them on the stove stirring the whole time until it starts to boil, and take it off and let it cool; chop in preserved lime peel with biscuits of bitter almonds and other biscuits, a little orange blossom water; mix all this with the cream, and take out the stick of cinnamon. Take eighteen fresh eggs, whip the whites as for meringues and put in twelve egg yolks while whipping them constantly, and empty in the prepared cream, and mix all this together. Rub a pot all over with good butter, and pour in your omelet, and put it in the oven; once it is cooked, turn it over on a plate and serve it hot as an entremets. This can be glazed, if you wish, with sugar and a hot shovel.
> (I:476, 1714, ed., cited in Alfred Franklin's *La Vie Privée d'Autrefois* (VI:71-72))

A modern cook would probably use a blowtorch (as for crème brulée) instead of a hot shovel to glaze this and the next dish.

Fried cream, garnished with peach beignets

The next dish in the last course is "1 dish of fried cream, garnished with peach beignets". Here are two recipes for fried cream:

> Take about a pint of milk, boil it on the fire, and mix in four egg yolks with a little flour. Once it is well blended, stir it all together on the stove until the cream is formed: put in a little salt, a little butter and some chopped lemon peel. Once it is cooked, flour your table and pour your Cream, so that it spreads out by itself: once it has cooled, it should look like a cooked omelet. Cut it into pieces, depending on the size you want, and fry them in good hot refined lard, being careful not to ruin them in the pan. Once it is browned, take it off; put powdered sugar and orange flower water on it. Lay it out in its dish, and having glazed it, if you wish, with a heated oven shovel, serve it hot. You can also, when this sort of cream is spread out on the table, have hot butter in your frying pan, and fry it like an omelet. When it is browned on one side, pour it into its dish, and move it gently around in the pan, to brown it on all sides. Sugar it, glaze it and serve it hot once again, all as an Entremets.
> (215-216, 1705 ed.)

> 253. To fry CREAM to eat hot.

> Take a pint of cream and boil it, three spoonfuls of London flour, mix'd with a little milk, put in three eggs, and beat them very well with the flour, a little salt, a spoonful or two of fine powder sugar, mix them very well; then put your cream to them on the fire and boil it; then beat two eggs more very well, and when you take your pan off the fire stir them in, and pour them into a large pewter dish, about half an inch thick; when it is quite cold cut it out in square bits, and fry it in butter, a light brown; as you fry them set them before the fire to keep hot and crisp, so dish them up with a little white wine, butter and sugar for your sauce, in a china cup, set it in the midst, and grate over some loaf sugar.
> Elizabeth Moxon, *English Housewifery Exemplified*, 1764

A beignet would seem simple enough, but La Varenne offers three different recipes for making beignets. The first of these can easily be used with slices of peach rather than apple or lemon peel:

How to make beignets or beignet.

Take a litron of fine flour, add to it three small cream cheeses, that is about .... [sic] of unskimmed cheese made the same day, break into it about three eggs, & beef marrow about the size of an egg, grated or chopped very fine, soak all this mixture & mix it well, while adding about four pints of white wine as needed, season this mixture with a pinch of fine salt, & with an ounce of powdered sugar, & this mixture or dough must be about as thick as cooked gruel; you may then add in apple cut into slices, or grated lemon peel cut into small pieces.

When this mixture is ready, heat refined lard, or butter, or oil, & when it is hot enough, stir your mixture with a spoon, take enough in the spoon, & drop it in the lard.

As soon as the beignets are cooked, take them out of the pan, & drain them, then put them in a bowl, powder them with sugar if you want, & sprinkle them with some drops of rosewater, or orange flower water.

Note that you can make the mixture or filling of your beignets more solid & reduce it to a soft dough, by putting in less wine, & this dough can be used for donkey's farts [*also known as "pets de nonne" - nun's farts – and by other such witty names*]; that is, instead of making common beignets, divide your dough into little round pieces the size of small hazelnuts, & cook them in refined lard or butter, or oils until they are fried brown.
La Varenne, *Le Cuisinier François*, Lyon, 1680 (301-302)

A stew of green truffles

The next dish in the third course of this model meal is a stew of green truffles. Truffles are generally black or white (or gray). But more than one cookbook includes a recipe for green truffles. It helps to know that in the period truffles were often sold dried or bottled. "Green" truffles were, apparently, simply fresh truffles, neither dried nor bottled.

Truffles, which did not become rare until much later on, appear frequently in 18th century recipes. In 1705, truffles were certainly prepared with no great ceremony:

TRUFFLES

The way of serving them that is most in vogue, is in court-bouillon; cooking them with white wine or claret, seasoned with salt, laurel, & pepper.

One can also put them on hot coals, half opening them, to put in a little salt and white pepper; & and having closed them again, cook them wrapped in moistened paper, over a hot fire which is not too brisk. Serve them in this way, on a folded napkin.

Or else, having peeled your truffles, cut them into slices, & brown them with melted lard or butter, & flour. Cook them with fines herbes, salt, nutmeg, pepper, & a little bouillon; & having thus simmered in a dish, to reduce the sauce, serve with Mutton juice & lemon.

Stews of Truffles & foie gras are also made, & Tarts…& for the…Collation at Lent, one can eat them dry with oil; all as entremets.
(490, 1705 ed.)

Several decades later, even stewing them seemed simple enough:

Truffle stew

    Once peeled & cut brown them on the fire with a half stick of butter or something else. Singe and moisten with a little bouillon, than some white veal stock. Boil a moment. Skim & serve.
Marin, *Les Dons de Comus*, 1763 (II:452)

The only complicated thing about this dish, really, would seem to be finding fresh truffles.

A dish of artichokes

The fourth of six dishes in the third service of this model meal is a simple dish of artichokes. The English writer Bradley says:

> It is a common practice in *France* to eat the small Heads of Artichokes raw, with Vinegar, Pepper, and Salt; the Method is to pull off the single Leaves, and dip the fleshy part of the Leaves into it and eat that. They are agreeably bitter, and create an Appetite.

This is preceded by this note on preserving them:

> Concerning the gathering, and ordering Artichokes for drying. In the gathering of Artichokes, observe, that the Leaves of what is call'd the Artichoke be pointing inwards, and lie close at the Top, for then the Bottom will be large and full; but if you find many of the Leaves of the Artichoke spread from the Top, then the Choke, or bristly part is shot so much, that it has drawn out much of the Heart of the Artichoke; and as the Flower comes forward, the more that grows, the thinner will be the Bottom, which is the best part of it.

> When you cut the Artichoke, cut it with a long Stalk, that when you use it you may clear it well of its Strings, which will else spoil the goodness of the Bottom, wherein the Strings will remain; to do this, lay the Artichoke upon a Table, and hold it down hard with one Hand, while with the other Hand you pull the Stalk hard up and down, till it quits the Artichoke, and will then pull away the Strings along with it; this being done, lay the Artichokes in Water for an Hour, and then put them into a Kettle of cold Water to boil, till they are tender enough to separate the Leaves and the Chokes from them. When this is done, lay the Hearts, or Bottoms upon a Cullender, or some other thing, to drain conveniently; then dry them upon a Wire Sieve, or Gridiron, in a gentle Oven, by degrees, till they are as hard as Wood. These will keep good twelve Months if they are laid by in a dry Place.

> When we want to use these for boiling, frying, or to accompany other Meats, we must put them into warm Water, often repeating it to them for eight and forty Hours, by which

means they will come to themselves, and be as good when they
come to be scalded as if they were fresh gather'd.
Bradley, *The Country Housewife and Lady's Director*, 1728 (111-
115)

Here is La Varenne's recipe for the dish:

Artichokes in Poivrade

Take artichokes which are tender, & cut them into quarters,
take out the choke, & the small leaves, also peel the underside, &
only leave the large leaves, & as they are peeled, throw them into
cold water to prevent them from blackening, & becoming bitter,
& when they are to be served, put them on a plate, or in a dish, in
the form of a pyramid: & sprinkle them with water. Put also on
the edge of the plate, pepper & salt beaten together.
 (117)

A dish of peas

The fifth of six dishes in the third service again seems simple: a dish of peas. Or maybe not so simple; the following is from an American cookbook:

Peas--Green Peas.

The *Crown Imperial* takes rank in point of flavor, they blossom, purple and white on the top of the vines, will run, from three to five feet high, should be set in light sandy soil only, or they run too much to vines.

The *Crown Pea*, is second in richness of flavor.

The *Rondeheval*, is large and bitterish.

Early Carlton, is produced first in the season—good.

Marrow Fats, green, yellow, and is large, easily cultivated, not equal to others.

Sugar Pea, needs no bush, the pods are tender and good to eat, easily cultivated.

Spanish Manratto, is a rich Pea, requires a strong high bush.

All Peas should be picked *carefully* from the vines as soon as dew is off, shelled and cleaned without water, and boiled immediately; they are thus the richest flavored.
Amelia Simmons, American Cookery: *The Art of Dressing Viands, Fish, Poultry, and Vegetables*, 1796

The same book gives this way to preserve them:

To keep Green Peas till Christmas

Take young peas, shell them, put them in a cullender to drain, then by a cloth four or five times double on a table, then spread them on, dry them very well, and have your bottles ready, fill them, cover them with mutton suet fat when it is a little soft; fill the necks almost to the top, cork them, tie a bladder and a leather over them and set them in a dry cool place.

Bonnefons' *Les Délices de la Campagne* (1655) goes on for several pages on the subject. Here is the start of that section:

On peas of all sorts.

> The younger & more excellent they are, the first to be eaten in spring are with the husk, to prepare them, put them to steam in a pot, with a little water, butter, fat, or lard, salt & a bit of spice according to taste; those which follow are husked, & put in steam like the preceding, fricasee them as well browning the butter, lard or fat, then throw them in with a little water to cook them, & season them with salt & spices, with a little parsley & spring onion chopped up fine together; if you want put in a few sprigs of thyme & marjoram to give them flavor, only tie them with thread to take them out whole then lay them in a dish, to thicken the sauce, sweet cream works wonderfully, but you must only put it in at the end...
> (147-148)

A dish of crayfish

The sixth of the six entrees for the third course is a dish of crayfish.

CRAYFISH

> They must be castrated [sic], that is pull out a gut that is in the tail, which is attached to the scale at the middle of the end of the tail, which after having been half turned, must be pulled & the gut comes out, after one cooks them in court-bouillon, that used to cook fish, can be used for crayfish; once cooked serve them dry on a plate, with a little peeled parsley, & dipped in vinegar on the top, to make a soup of crayfish, one takes the large shell of the back off, which one fills with fish hash, & one peels the feet & the tails, which are put to cook together in a pot with the bouillon from the large pot [*which held simmering bones, scales, tails, etc.*]; to serve them put them on simmered bread [*simmered in soup, says the* Larousse Gastronomique], putting the feet & the tails in the middle, with a little border of chopped parsley around the plate."\
Bonnefons, *Les délices de la campagne*, 1655 (341-342,326)

What appears to be a court-bouillon is given for carp at the start of the article on "Fish":

> Butter, salt, vinegar, onion, lemon peel, or orange, spices, a lot of wine and a quart of water...A half-court-bouillon is made having emptied the carp without scaling it & without cutting it, put it in the cauldron with the same sauce... & add capers, plums, Damask grapes, case grapes [*'de quaisse' - a rare type from the south of France*], Corinth grapes, pine nut & pistachios: instead of laying it out on slices of bread, put in spice bread. (322-323)

Two hors d'oeuvres

Fried animelles

Animelles will be better known to Americans as "Rocky Mountain Oysters" - to name only one of a series of winking puns, all probably covers for the discomfort prompted by the idea of eating any male's... well, maleness: hanging beef, calf fries, tendergroin...In other words, testicles.

It seems these were prized under Louis XV, if hard to find, and still served in at least one restaurant in Paris in the mid-nineteenth century:

> ANIMELLES. Thus are called the apparent signs of a ram's virility. It is a food with a pronounced, but sweet and frank, taste. Dispensaries [*recipe and formula books*] from the time of Louis XV show that animelles were then a sought after delicacy, and that an excessive price was paid for them. All sorts of diaphoretic virtues are attributed to them in the highest degree; but, whatever the case, it remains a succulent and tonic food. It is still used and much appreciated in Spanish cooking, where the best way to prepare them is in fried batter with a sauce of lemon juice, wild mint and hot pepper. On must first as a preliminary be careful to divide each of one's animelles into six pieces, and to have marinated them for an hour or two with lemon, salt and long pepper. It cannot always be found at Paris butchers', because there is an industrial establishment in this city which absorbs them; but people who are counseled the use of them, or who might have the fantasy of eating them, can send to have them from this same establishment, that is at *the Spanish restaurant of sir Lauer, rue Neuve-des-Petits-Champs, n. 35*, where are always to be found, at the dinner hour, fresh and carefully prepared animelles.
> *Dictionnaire Général de la cuisine française ancienne et moderne*, 1835 (31)

Was this "delicacy" omitted from most period cookbooks because of its price, or for other reasons? Here some rare recipes for the dish from the eighteenth century:

Ways to prepare Animelles

Cut the Animelles in pieces, four or eight, take off the skin, put on a little grated salt, flour them, put them in hot frying fat, & they should be very crunchy when you take them out. Serve hot as an entremets.

Another way

Soak flour in beer or wine; add in a half glass of oil & of salt. The Animelles being half-fried, put them in this dough, put them immediately back in the frying fat. Once they are fried, garnish them with fried parsley. Serve hot.

Third way

Marinate the Animelles with slices of onion, parsley, pepper, clove, vinegar, a little bouillon, cut as usual. Put them in beaten eggs, bread them. Fry them, and serve with fried parsley.
Dictionnaire des alimens, vins et liqueurs, 1750 (I:84)

Even those readers who inexplicably do not want to eat (or even prepare) animelles might find these recipes work nicely with, say, scallops.

A dish of ramekins

What goes with fried testicles?

The second hors d'oeuvre, presumably served at the same time as the preceding dish, is a dish of ramekins - which can be anything from little unsweetened cheese pastries to something like Welsh Rabbit to a kind of poor man's soufflé.

This, apparently, was one dish eighteenth century cooks paired with fried "signs of virility."

There are different ways to prepare ramekins (ramequins). The *Dons de Comus*'s version uses anchovies:

Ramekins

Put in a pot a little water, about half a glass, & a lump of butter. When this begins to boil put in flour as for a royal dough. When it is done, put in four eggs. Mix it all together well, & put in two anchovies & Brie and Gruyere cheese, & some coarse pepper. Grate well. Grease small pate molds, & form your ramekins. Cook them & serve hot.
Les Dons de Comus (III:122)

Royal dough

Put a pint of water, a little salt and a quarter pound of butter in a pot: boil a moment, then put in flour until it forms a well blended dough, & keep stirring it until it comes free of the pot, then take it off the fire, & put in lemon gratings & eggs one after the other, as much as the dough can absorb: (as can be seen when it begins to stick to the finger) then use it.
(III:12)

For something fancier:

Ramekin soufflés

Make a very light little piece of royal dough the size of two eggs. Put in the mortar with twice as much good butter, parsley chopped up fine, a half-quarter of very mild Brie cheese, & a quarter pound of grated Gruyere, also very mild. Grate it all together & put in five egg yolks one after the other, & the whites separately, to beat them. When everything is well grated, mix in your egg whites. Line pie plates with very fine puff pastry dough; put about two inches of your mixture in these with a spoon. Cook them in a hot oven to sear them, & after let them cook slowly. You will see them rise with the eye.

When they are cooked and settled, serve them quite hot. It only takes a quarter of an hour to cook them. Be careful to be able to serve them when they come out of the oven. (III:123-124)

CPSIA information can be obtained
at www.ICGtesting.com
Printed in the USA
LVHW111237280419
615846LV00001B/143/P

9 781434 829856